Notes from the Last Age

by

José Chapa Valle

FLOWERSONG
PRESS

FlowerSong Press
McAllen, Texas 78501
Copyright © 2020 by José Chapa Valle

ISBN: 978-1-7345617-5-3

Published by FlowerSong Press
in the United States of America.
www.flowersongpress.com

Set in Adobe Garamond Pro

Cover Artwork by David Figueroa / @figudam
Typeset and design by Matthew Revert matthewrevert.com

No part of this book my be reproduced without written permission from the publisher.

All inquiries and permission requests should be addressed to the publisher.

Some poems in this book appeared first in Star*Line, The Central American Literary Review and La Bloga.

To Andrea, translator of the celestial.

I. The Beholder

11. The End
12. Wandering Samurai
13. Recalling a portrait during spring
14. Ascendant
15. Midnight Seeker
16. The Gate
17. Ghost of the 1850's
19. Morrowind
20. Vishnu sings for a specific woman
22. And then
24. Missouri City, Texas, in a far tomorrow
25. Notes from the last age
26. Seer
28. To any astronauts still stranded on planet earth
30. Self-concious

II. I saw the tree salivate

33. Anchor
35. The nothing
36. Shadow Brook
38. Many sides
39. Photograph
40. Loud blood lay spilt
41. At surgery
42. Breeder
43. Reunion
44. Recurring lightning

III. Intimate dictionary

47. Idioma
48. Espejos
49. Renuncia
50. Patria
51. Mármol
52. Adobe
53. Jaula
54. Pavura
55. Naturaleza
56. Axioma
57. Veladora
58. Ceguera
59. Brujeria
60. Cancion

The Beholder

The End

Raw was the first word. Naked
until the trees grew, until the ground
looked at the sky
and reached for it. Antlers of earth
gave way to wolf packs, and at their cry
snow fell, beckoned. Aroused, wet,
the first word grew, surrounded by more
and more.

Till raging ape
killed raging ape
and turned. Raw were their eyes
so the first word trembled.
Raw was the angry water
they spilled on the ground.
Raw was the stump of the tree.

Wandering samurai

Mirikitani rose
with an atomic vision of bursting persimmons
lingering in his mind.

Still soaked in the night's rain
he gathered his gear:
a brush sheathed in ink, a handful of seeds
to plant in the wasteland, to shatter the grey absolute;
photographs with fading faces
and a skin of captured water.

In the clamor of his loneliness
he looked at the landscape, at the work that lay before him.

Unending, red
rolling hills of rooftops,
unforgiving, harsh,

where all things
were created equal.

Recalling a portrait during spring

The first sword I ever held
purred in its black sheathe.

It knew me like an intimate ancestor,
a ghost of the bones that carry me.

It took me out to the gardens
and drew my face in the sand.

Only the waters of the stream, restless,
had ever shown me my face before.

Then a child, now a man,
I still remember.

Ascendant

My friend sat down to meditate,
center of the dancefloor:
elbows and knees grazed him
as did the tight aromas
and the laughing gaze of strangers.
All around him: revelry, fun.
His eyelids trembled
containing what gleam, we do not know.
Certain, unreachable,
he felt the impulse and complied
serene amid the noise.

I went about the party
and fell in love, got hired,
made plans for mortgage.

Now I search for him
in a field of empty bottles
and forgotten names.

Midnight Seeker

Bright silence of winter,
moonlight frozen between stones,
black ice breathing beneath boots,
she recites the invocation.

Ancient words
burn in the black night
all flecked with silver,
torn from her lips to the hungry eye,
wrenched from her soul by the ceaseless want.

She sees clearly:
rotten gate, wooden key,
deep mountains behind.
She turns it
and all the names of the fires in the sky
jamble her mind, burning true,
unmeant for speech.

Dark morning. Her frosted figure
dawns dead with a smile.

The Gate

Was it born from the light
like a shadow,
or from the brightness banished
for the faceless dream it wore?
Woven branches
rotting around its skin,
crown of muck.
Charred roots for legs.
Was it born or forsaken
knowing all the unknown?

Ghost of the 1850's

     I

She sent a letter,
there was an Ocean in there
and a Mind that drunk it whole.

There was a round Presence,
huge, heavy,
drop of dew
on Sycamore leaves.

     II

It read like this
but not as rudely,
written on wildflowers
within a box
wrapped in lace.

     III

These are some things she did not mention:

The light, brownish color beneath a horse's shoe,
the vibrant Circles of a passing bike
gleaming silver but only heard,
the alligator on the curb
shedding moonlight and chills.

    IV
She dotted the eyes with visions of buzzing clouds
and trees so darkly arranged
their leaves were countless crows,
dreaming.

Morrowind

Ruins,
red, rage-misted skies,
wounded crowns of rock
circling groves.

Such sights around Balmora.
Lover, let me tell you more.

Vishnu sings for a specific woman

In cities of ashen shine you pucker lips
too lush to be anything but yours.

Winding through windows
the wind chimes slowly,
mingles the threads of your brown hair
with the voice of horses wild, unseen,

brought from the steppes of common place heaven
to the machinations of light that surrounds you,
city-dwelling fox of the fiery tome
of unreason.

In this catastrophic miracle that is my dream,
in this cosmic clutter of symbols
and names

where histories are meaningless
and bones turn to stone
and stones fly
launched from the small hands of children;
in this reckless melody first heard
so many dreams ago, this composition
of burning wolves and howling jellyfish,

random shapes unexpectedly take form
the nonsense
is all laid out
and spoken with measure. Jungles cease to be

a water paint haze
and become jungles, teeming of song's true form

when from the moisture of a shower
you emerge, deciphering.

And then

As our lips meet the rough edge of the cup
where pulque waits, full bodied,
cities rise in rebellion over the turning
of a key in the door of power: revolts against masters of automation
and maintenance.
Veracruz daylight gives the establishment
a hue of earth unshaken, plastic tables in a backyard
set and from the window the madam looks to see
if we need more.
Ancient spires rip through farmlands
like needles rising from the inside of a wound
to seal a suture. Waves crash against walls
that bear, in glyphs, our history. Our moment is forgotten,
the thirsty ocean does not read our delight.
We laugh at the ones who wouldn't join us
in the expedition through a tropical town,
through two weeks when we all chose names
unaccustomed to the shackles of our voice.
An expedition that ends here in the pulque shop.
We eye each other,
wonder if it would be fair to the rest of the world
should we decide to start a commune. Should we collapse into an orgy
in the courtyards of the wind.
Fire licks the marble of vast libraries, tomes trembling on shelves,
wires retreating like wax from vengeful heat.
Beautiful people crowd the highways
and their descendents huddle in ruined structures.
All comes to a conclusion like a heartbeat, like a universe,
and prepares to start again

but we can only know the fun we're having
and how it seems our meeting was a thing of fate,
an encounter meant to be.

Not one of us sees what is happening now.

Missouri City, Texas, in a far tomorrow

Stillness in the hall of a great house.
The creature glows in a bright yellow
with red clouds moving across her skin.
Her eyes fixed on a twinkling arrangement.
It refracts the light of her glow
and tinges yellow, red, obsidian orange
the darkness around them both.
A chandelier. She eyes the crystals
as they click together, slowly.
She disturbed their ancient space
in exploration. The device and she, they are nebula in the depth:
a sunken star, shattered in light.

She sneaks three of her arms around the chandelier,
grips tight on a strand of crystals: they taste unknown like ice.
She rips them free
and instantly her shapeless escape
propels her from the great house to the open, ruined world.

The strand of crystals will hang in her den
for her babes to marvel.
And when all of them dream, brilliant,
motionless, filling the cavern with light,
the crystals will translate, unseen.

Notes from the last age

There was a station that sexy animals set ablaze.
A golden telescope
that sent many images from its wayward trajectory:
colossal magnesium clouds
in the shape of a meditating human.
There was an artificial comet created in a far corner
by some glass technologies.
A huge, planet-sized sculpture of a pocket watch
filled with sand.
There was a signal
transmitted through telling darkness,
decrypted too late by the stubborn
and vastly rich nations of earth:

It is a heart. It is a blinking mind.

Seer

I
I've never seen a comet in my life,
passing through days that fall on rooftops
and warzones, through nights
when all I regret is being wise
and having a boredom of work that rots my teeth.

I've been through cities, countrysides,
watching with eyes that were eyes in the universe:
blessed. I've seen the roads that wind through jungles,
a green that fills and fathoms speech. I've been to Veracruz.

Though I've never seen a comet
my eyes are filled to bursting.

II

Without owning a telescope I graduate astronomer,
I ignore the laws that bind galaxies
but know their inner workings in my sleep, find them
similar to cells of my own body.
Find them similar to fires lit and then remembered
after many years, the fires only, bare
with no one or anything around them.
Find them small and meaningless like me.

These galaxies arranged in curtains
of light almost chiseled into being,
carved out of a darkness by our sculpting eyes;
these galaxies arranged in walls, argent hieroglyphs,
I read them in my sleep.
Their silent poetry wakes me.

To any astronauts still stranded on Planet Earth

Avoid attending parties
and if you fail
lurk in the corners, smile precisely
like a sniper,
do not dance
but rock a nervous leg.
Cringe at the sound of your name
mumbled by secretive teeth,
look at the beautiful
and look at the ground right after.

Go to supermarkets at the hour
in which your mind lights up with supernovas,
at that hour love,
at that hour write.

Parks will extend before you
like plains of daggers pulled from ribs.
Streets will extend before you
like flowers of ink drawn from the ground
to write on your back the word "foreigner".

Hurry from the workplace
to your private prison
without touching a soul, as is the custom.
Keep to yourself
the secrets of elsewhere.

Earthlings can never understand

that sometimes light takes shape.
To them the universe is a creation
or an accident. They cannot fathom middle grounds.

So avoid their parties,
speak about yourself as you would speak
of something you don't understand
and secretly recall the silver streams, fertile deserts,
that wait for your return.

Self-Conscious

I begin here. My existence is at once quantifiable
and unknowable. Contradiction is my nature.
I am beautiful because I lack sight
yet tell this vision: elephants drink lotus flowers
in a panicked river.
This is my end, as close as I come to it.

I saw the tree salivate

Anchor

The truly solitary
don't know what to say to their mothers
in the sky's cold rooms.

Secretly they tire of their own kids:
laughing water birds
that crash into walls and keep laughing.

The solitary have lovers who ruin themselves
of reasons they should be together,
of nude selfies
sent nervously.
They don't promise anything, but they feel a certain
warm emptiness.

They show respect:
nod to police,
curse with coworkers,
look away from the beautiful.
Surrounded,

they only wish
to be truly alone.
Their hair starts to fade
and their family,
they are afraid
to be truly alone.

Perhaps their eyes move rapidly

in that dark electricity magenta and green,
towering visions;
or perhaps they don't sleep.

But the swollen hours of night
are their only freedom.
White noise
reverberates in their bones.
Wine or true mescal
defuse them.
Daybreak catches them biting
a hard coin.

They are the ones who think about crying
at funerals. Who become teachers, firefighters,
keepers of open land, dieticians and bankers.
Who only wish they were smart enough
for space exploration.

They'd strand themselves out there
but no further than the moon;
what would be life without view of the ocean?

The Nothing

Of the soccer ball grazing the post
and streets all brimming with darkness.
Of the hands tied together in secret,
the swollen windows of an afternoon home
erupting with quiet.
The overwhelming gratitude of birds
who surround us with flight, unhunted.
Of broken light cascading onto a naked beach,
of naked ash blown suddenly away
to another, abandoned, time.
Full-of-speech rooms
empty with words, unrecognized
battlefields. Eyes that met in the tumult
and quickly forgot.
Also the nothing we challenge
with every rise from the bed.

Shadow Brook

    I

"I know these clouds from somewhere else," said Ivory
up in the tree house between two jails,
"Jet planes flew through them   the night a window hit me."

She touched the leg of a stranger
as her skinny friend assured us that mice
will live on people if a certain bond is made;
that you just have to get used to their crawling.

We could hear a train way back
behind our laughter and the birds
that panicked revving engines;
beyond the leaves that rustled sharp.

We could hear it clearly
like a photograph.

But the four us of only wanted to stay high
over the rooftops of the jails in Shadow Brook,
familiar clouds
still torn surrounding us.

    II

Each of us sat however we could
when the ground began to rise.

The mouse knelt
pleading "look at the bars,
they're white and cool".

The stranger kept a hand between his legs
reclining on the planks.

Ivory laid on the side of her own body.
I saw the tree salivate,

sitting in meditation, I saw the tree bark seeping.

Many sides

Jack the price of vital drugs,
label one life over another,
insure the darkness of the wells
beyond its value when all our bones are uninsured,
trap the bridge between worlds
with an electrified welcome mat;
demolish sanctuaries
to build banks,
deny access
to charge fees.
Give unjust orders, follow them.
Give themselves bonuses.
Give generously
to the Rotting God of Confusion.
Plan obsolescence. Plan surviving their nuclear mistakes.
Their slow boiling of the seas. Plan profiting.

And yet only one side
suffers.

Photograph

Soldiers crossing a forest
in the dark mist of daybreak,
leaves stick to their weapons.

They wear their helmets as an afterthought,
they hang from their temples unlike crowns.

Moving through a forest they can never know,
moving slowly without making a sound,
moving
until their loud blood lay spilt.

Loud Blood Lay Spilt

Rows of white
with but a name chiseled;
what are they
chanting in harmony?

At Surgery

The brain is grooved like a dried raisin,
with a symmetry that recalls rolling hills
or the close up of a wheat stalk. A lushness.

In its vulnerable stillness
it cries for the warmth of the skull:
it gleams, and almost quivers at the sound of tools.

It will never be a soldier again.

Breeder

An acre of Texas
with a single rusted shack.
Brown wires in the dark yard, squaring
kennels for these images:

two Blue Heelers
and their pups,
two Rottweilers
full of scars.

A still Doberman,
the worms that slowly
ate his living eyes.

Reunion

Don't I know you from Babylon?
There was a drowning music behind the walls,

blue light swirling of smoke and laughter, the lingering taste of mescaline
and bodies dancing all around. Half naked
they twirled about, beautifully obscene, appalling and perfect.

I think it was your eyes
the eyes that marveled most, I can still see them
deep in the well of young desire, open like mouths
that only knew hunger. And your hands I think
were the hands that felt the most.

Not like they are now,
having left the velvet city:
ragged, still, uneventfully resigned.

Yes, it must have been Babylon,
the bar where we first met.

Recurring Lightning

A full circle on a window that frosted
over a look outside, drawn with a tip.

Revelatory, round, fading back
into the unexpected cold.
Suddenly remembered, of all things,
gone
like the trees on the lawn, like the brick mailbox
your brother crashed his bike into.

More than the circle itself,
all it contained. The intimacies of that year,
the pitch and tone of the voices
which called out in laughter
from the living room that is now empty.

More than the circle
its fleeting existence on the glass,
its permanence in you.

Intimate Dictionary

Idioma

English for business, the fucking of others and war;
the colder, monumental poetry.
For the toasting to drugs and also
for insidious deceit we know will be known.
English for the reign of liberty, dreams
of how people should govern themselves.

Spanish for council with dogs, prayer,
remembering exiles and exiled times;
cursing to hell the preacher and his hand in the pot,
singing songs about weed, almost weeping.
Spanish for the moments after sex,
when we try to say something about the wind
without it blowing us away.

Espejos

I despise their sheen,
the way artificial light
catches them naked;
their silver something that cannot be seen.

They multiply into infinity
when faced with each other.
They force me to find them
in the narrow halls of a sweet home,
in the dark of the eyes that see me.

They pull my gaze from the beating sky
onto a street where they lay shattered,
reflecting the bellies of beetles.

Renuncia

I'm done with the bodies of earth,
with this flesh that hustles in darkness
and thrives at the gripping release.
I'm done with the loving abandon,
the violence we share
which opens the night to new days:
necessary key brought to it's breaking.
Done with the needing
what never was mine or enough.

So I'm going away, reaching out
for new things. Drifting
toward the celestial.

Patria

My soul listened,

heard that it was lost
in search of a great treasure
and that certainly, one day, it would be found.

Now I know I am American.

Mármol

Rows of white
with but a name chiseled;
what are they
chanting in harmony?

Adobe

I look out the timeless window
to a world that drowns in it,
a sphere that expands and contracts
like the heart of hate.

Cacti grow on mud houses
from the walls and roofs.
They cling to the homes that spawned them.
Years after doors were ignited,
windows vandalized,
they proudly remain.

Jaula

No dreams among these elephants, they lay awake
in a concrete room, huddled, surrounded.

In their morning chains they will straddle
as if walking a long walk

to their beginning.

Pavura

This feeling, I know I've seen it in canines
when they understand that certain legs will not be climbed,
seen it in children who playing in the earth
found bones
too familiar in shape and smell.

The back has a dream of a thousand bees
buzzing in a block of ice.
The voice buckles

when what you fear
is also loved, respected.
The mentor whose daughter you shamed,
the government,
your own grandfather
calling from a casket buried somewhere
in the cruel blue of day:

I'm disappointed.

Naturaleza

Enamored by the idea of the wilds,
self-sustainable lifestyles,
meditations off the grid,
I face the faces I could not live without.

They are few
and of short names.

So I face the things I could not live without.
Peanut butter, video games, imported mexican beer,
the rush of blood that fills the white
of my two eyes after a smoke;
cold, even, unnatural floors
on which to lay.

I am not cut out for the lifestyle
of the mountain men.
My two hands lead me to the bookshelf
and pick out a slender volume.

I open a random page
and return to my own wilderness.

Axioma

Death dislikes famine
because the hungry die weak
and make poor dinner.

She lives for the suddenly taken, the roasted,
the jumpers.

Veladora

Wallow the wings
of a fluttering light,
silence
darkens the room.

Ceguera

An unkindness of ravens blessed me today,
they landed in the snow
and fooled around for a while; a dozen ravens
rolling and searching, digging in the white ground.
I heard someone laugh.

An unkindness of ravens
blessed me today.

Brujeria

White birds live, featherless birds
hideous among leaves, on the slim branches of a tree
hiding. Lethality in its roots, and in the house it shades

a lunacy moon-viewed, a rambling stereo cat
shrouded like a light blue cloud.

While crows rejoice, medallions yet un-shining.

Canción

My dad was shot in the back
as he walked out of a bar.

I was waiting for him on the sidewalk
across the street,
and when he fell
I ran as fast as the bullet
but I could never reach him.

We buried him in his only pair of boots,
which my mother cleaned before the ceremony.

In my whole life
it was the first time I saw them
shine.

Bio:

Jose Chapa Valle authored *Pájaros de Pólvora* and *Sospecha de un Viaje Astral*. His work has been sighted in literary journals across Latin America and the United States, including Star*Line, Acentos Review, Luvina, Tierra Adentro and Pliego 16. He was a grantee of the Instituto Coahuilense de Cultura in 2010, under the Jovenes Creadores category. He currently resides in Houston, Texas, where he cultivates a beautiful anonymity.

www.ingramcontent.com/pod-product-compliance
Lightning Source LLC
Chambersburg PA
CBHW071321080526
44587CB00018B/3314